ADDICTION RECOVERY DIY

Conquer Your Drug or Alcohol Addiction At Home

VOLUME ONE

K.J. Gordon

5D Media Publishing
orders@5dmedia.org
www.5Dmedia.org

Ordering Information: Quantity sales. Special discounts are available on quantity purchases by corporations, associations, and others. For details, contact the publisher at the address above.
Orders by U.S. trade bookstores and wholesalers. Please contact Big Distribution: orders@5dmedia.org or visit www.5DMedia.org.
Printed in the United States of America

Addiction Recovery DIY / K.J. Gordon

ISBN-10:0-9989217-3-4
ISBN-13:978-0-9989217-3-0
First Edition

DEDICATION

This workbook is dedicated to anyone struggling with an addiction or dependence to drugs or alcohol. It can be utilized alone or while completing the "Addiction Recovery DIY" Video series.

While Addiction Recovery at home is possible for some with focus and discipline, others may need some professional help along the way. And there is nothing wrong with that.

If you think you may need additional help, or just someone to talk to, Direct Message us on Instagram @AddictionRecoveryDIY or email support@foreverfight.com.

CONTENTS

1

FOCUS ON YOUR RECOVERY

Congratulations! You did it! You have taken your first step towards Recovery. Now, prepare yourself mentally for what's ahead. Your new life in sobriety will require a total lifestyle change. Decide now that you are ready to change aspects of yourself, your social circle, your routine, and even your eating and sleeping habits.

Over the next week, we will work on taking you from stuck, to unstuck, to making a plan for your future.

We will utilize the time tested and proven tool of journaling to help you identify the factors in your life that must change for you to achieve a successful recovery.

Are you ready? Let's get started!

◈ ◈ ◈ ◈ ◈ ◈

2

SCHEDULING YOUR TIME

First I need you to make a promise to yourself. That you will effectively utilize your personal time over the next 7 days to focus on your Recovery. This will include watching reading this guidebook or watching the videos, making key constructive observations about your life, and completing each journal activity.

Once you make this promise, it will be harder to procrastinate and avoid making excuses for yourself. You will be less impulsive, as you've planned your time.

Organization and scheduling will take you from where you are to where you need to be. It will

be harder to forget the positive activities, and easier to forget the harmful ones. You will achieve Sobriety and conquer your goals, one day at a time.

On the following pages, fill out your schedule for the next 7 days. The times you are at work, at school or any other commitments you have that do not include drug or alcohol use. If possible, schedule hours of sleep for yourself.

"I'm not married. Have no kids. So for about 5 years I got off work everyday at 5, and would go to our local hangout for dinner, and of course drink all night. I would come home and pass out at 11 or 12, and was up by 7 the next morning to do it all over again. So really from 5pm during the week and basically all day on the weekends I didn't do anything productive with my time."-Sean M., Maine

EXAMPLES

DAY 1:

Monday

12:00AM	Sleep
1:00 AM	Sleep
2:00 AM	Sleep
3:00 AM	Sleep
4:00 AM	Sleep
5:00 AM	Sleep
6:00 AM	Sleep
7:00 AM	Breakfast
8:00 AM	Drive to Work
9:00 AM	Work
10:00AM	Work
11:00AM	Work
12:00PM	Work / Lunch
1:00 PM	Work
2:00 PM	Work
3:00 PM	Work
4:00 PM	Work
5:00 PM	Leave Work
6:00 PM	
7:00 PM	Dinner
8:00 PM	
9:00 PM	
10:00PM	
11:00PM	Sleep

DAY 3:

Friday

12:00AM	work
1:00 AM	work
2:00 AM	work
3:00 AM	work
4:00 AM	work
5:00 AM	work
6:00 AM	
7:00 AM	sleep
8:00 AM	sleep
9:00 AM	sleep
10:00AM	sleep
11:00AM	sleep
12:00PM	sleep
1:00 PM	sleep
2:00 PM	sleep
3:00 PM	
4:00 PM	
5:00 PM	
6:00 PM	
7:00 PM	
8:00 PM	Leave for work
9:00 PM	work
10:00PM	work
11:00PM	work

Day 1:

Day 2:

12:00 AM	
1:00 AM	
2:00 AM	
3:00 AM	
4:00 AM	
5:00 AM	
6:00 AM	
7:00 AM	
8:00 AM	
9:00 AM	
10:00 AM	
11:00 AM	
12:00 PM	
1:00 PM	
2:00 PM	
3:00 PM	
4:00 PM	
5:00 PM	
6:00 PM	
7:00 PM	
8:00 PM	
9:00 PM	
10:00 PM	
11:00 PM	

Day 3:

12:00 AM	_____
1:00 AM	_____
2:00 AM	_____
3:00 AM	_____
4:00 AM	_____
5:00 AM	_____
6:00 AM	_____
7:00 AM	_____
8:00 AM	_____
9:00 AM	_____
10:00 AM	_____
11:00 AM	_____
12:00 PM	_____
1:00 PM	_____
2:00 PM	_____
3:00 PM	_____
4:00 PM	_____
5:00 PM	_____
6:00 PM	_____
7:00 PM	_____
8:00 PM	_____
9:00 PM	_____
10:00 PM	_____
11:00 PM	_____

Day 4:

12:00 AM _____

1:00 AM _____

2:00 AM _____

3:00 AM _____

4:00 AM _____

5:00 AM _____

6:00 AM _____

7:00 AM _____

8:00 AM _____

9:00 AM _____

10:00 AM _____

11:00 AM _____

12:00 PM _____

1:00 PM _____

2:00 PM _____

3:00 PM _____

4:00 PM _____

5:00 PM _____

6:00 PM _____

7:00 PM _____

8:00 PM _____

9:00 PM _____

10:00 PM _____

11:00 PM _____

Day 5:

12:00 AM	
1:00 AM	
2:00 AM	
3:00 AM	
4:00 AM	
5:00 AM	
6:00 AM	
7:00 AM	
8:00 AM	
9:00 AM	
10:00 AM	
11:00 AM	
12:00 PM	
1:00 PM	
2:00 PM	
3:00 PM	
4:00 PM	
5:00 PM	
6:00 PM	
7:00 PM	
8:00 PM	
9:00 PM	
10:00 PM	
11:00 PM	

Day 6:

Time	
12:00 AM	
1:00 AM	
2:00 AM	
3:00 AM	
4:00 AM	
5:00 AM	
6:00 AM	
7:00 AM	
8:00 AM	
9:00 AM	
10:00 AM	
11:00 AM	
12:00 PM	
1:00 PM	
2:00 PM	
3:00 PM	
4:00 PM	
5:00 PM	
6:00 PM	
7:00 PM	
8:00 PM	
9:00 PM	
10:00 PM	
11:00 PM	

Day 7:

12:00 AM _____

1:00 AM _____

2:00 AM _____

3:00 AM _____

4:00 AM _____

5:00 AM _____

6:00 AM _____

7:00 AM _____

8:00 AM _____

9:00 AM _____

10:00 AM _____

11:00 AM _____

12:00 PM _____

1:00 PM _____

2:00 PM _____

3:00 PM _____

4:00 PM _____

5:00 PM _____

6:00 PM _____

7:00 PM _____

8:00 PM _____

9:00 PM _____

10:00 PM _____

11:00 PM _____

Now, go back and circle all the times you are available. These are the times you will focus on your Recovery. Write them down here.

I WILL FOCUS ON MY RECOVERY DURING THE FOLLOWING DAYS AND TIMES

Day 1:

Day 2:

Day 3:

Day 4:

Day 5:

Day 6:

Day 7:

Write down the current date and time below as your "Start" time. Then, write down the date and time exactly one week from now. This is your completion deadline. From this point forward you will hold yourself accountable for completing the first step on your Passage to Recovery by this date and time. This will be a huge accomplishment. And you should feel very proud of yourself for setting this goal.

Start: _____

Completion Deadline: _____

◈ ◈ ◈ ◈ ◈

3

EVERYTHING IN THE UNIVERSE IS CONNECTED

Staying stuck emotionally and physically will only bring you closer to using drugs or alcohol. Life is about movement and change. If you stay stuck, life events will just occur to you, taking away your control. Understand you are instrumental in what happens in your life. Together we will make realistic goals, and proceed forward. We will utilize past experiences as motivators to not use. You will start allowing others to love you, even when it is difficult to love yourself. These videos are just a guide to take you from point A to point B. You are in control. You are making the change. No one is telling you what to do. This is a lifestyle change, not a temporary fix.

For right now, chose to try this sober thing out. After completing this video series you can choose to go back to your old lifestyle, it's your choice. But if you chose to stay on the road to recovery, positive things will start happening to you.

Now, ask yourself for forgiveness because you are no longer the same person.

Let's Start with a practice exercise. Write a paragraph about how life will be now that you are sober, then proceed to the next video.

❖　❖　❖　❖　❖　❖

4

SAYING GOODBYE TO YOUR ADDICTION

It is time to say goodbye to your addiction. Recovery is a long process that is mentally and physically draining on your mind, body and spirit The relationship you have with drugs or alcohol is more harmful than any other relationship you will have. If you are ready to achieve sobriety, it is time to say goodbye to your addiction.

The first thing I want you to do is write a private goodbye letter to your addiction. Let it know that you are letting go and moving on. Recount all the bad things that happened to get rid of your anger, shame, and resentment. All the bad behavior and poor judgment calls. Do not rush through this activity. Take your time.

Every time you consider reusing you will reread this letter to yourself. It will remind you of the time in your life that you don't want to revisit. Every time you think you can use, this letter will remind you of the harmful consequences of that decision. Once you are done, rip out the pages, place them in an envelope, and in put it somewhere that you can access when you need the reminder.

Goodbye To My Addiction
By:_____

❖ ❖ ❖ ❖ ❖ ❖

5

IDENTIFYING YOUR FEARS

Everyone fears something - failure, success, or even being unable to pay bills. Fear makes you stuck and incapable of moving in any direction. Feelings of entrapment caused by fear is a major contributor to drug and alcohol abuse and addiction. You can overcome any fear. But first you must identify what they are.

Write down the top 10 things you fear. This could include being alone, never being married or having kids. A fear of getting fired, or of leaving your comfort zone for a job or for school. A fear of emotional pain or of being alone. Take at least ten minutes to complete this list.

1) _____

2) _____

3) _____

4) _____

5) _____

6) _____

7) _____

8) _____

9) _____

10) _____

Look at your list. While it is healthy to have some rational fears, most fears can be crippling to your progress and need to be dissected and overcome. Look at each of your fears and think of ways in which they can be overcome.

"I was first prescribed Pain Pills by a pain doctor after hurting my back in a car accident. Eight years later I couldn't stop . They gave me the energy I felt I needed to be a good mother to my 3 kids. I knew I needed to stop using, but was scared of detoxing, and becoming a horrible mother. It sounds kind of silly now. But That's how I saw it.

My husband begged me to go to Rehab. Our insurance through his job would cover the cost, but I still found excuses because I was scared. He would tell me I deserved the time to focus on myself. But I worried about the kids, and the dog. My mother in law even offered to help. But it was never enough. My fears were totally irrational. A friend helped me realize that, Then I got help. " ***-Samantha, Texas***

Remember these fears as you go on to the next activity which will help you better understand how these fears actively affect your daily life.

6

24 HOURS OF OBSERVATION

The next activity will require you to really dig deep and observe your life. A crucial step in Recovery is seeing who and what triggers you to use drugs and alcohol. It could be food, work, an event, or certain friends or family members.

For the next 24 hours, I want you to record everything you do. Every hour, write down the time, where you are, what you are eating, what you are doing, and how you are feeling. Pay close attention to who and what effects your mood and behavior. Include any exercise or long walks; the events or gatherings you attend, and the food and activities associated with them.

Keep in mind you will most likely be doing some of these activities sober for the first time in a while. If something makes you want to use, write it down. If you need more space than provided in this section, utilize the pages provided at the end of the workbook. Most people pretty much keep the same daily, weekly, and even annual routines. This is how you become stuck doing the same thing over and over again. We will utilize this dissection of your daily routine to learn what your old habits are, and how to break them.

Really take this seriously because you are now in the driver's seat. Now go figure out what is getting you stuck on a daily bases, and how you can get unstuck. In at least 24 hours from now, you can proceed to the next video.

24 HOURS OF OBSERVATION

◈ ◈ ◈ ◈ ◈ ◈

7

ANALYSIS OF YOUR 24 HOURS OF OBSERVATION

Welcome back from your 24 hours of reflection and journaling. How do you feel? Self-assessment can be draining, so take a deep breath and know that you have just made a giant leap towards your Recovery. Now that you have familiarized yourself with journaling, the remaining exercises will be much easier for you.

Now open your notes from the past 24 hours; and read through them and see if you identify any key contributors to your past drug and alcohol use. Circle them all, and write them down on the next page. Identify and add your cravings and triggers. These are the things that you saw, heard or smelled, that made you want to take action to do something. Addiction is all about these urges. And Recovery is all about reprogramming yourself away from them.

Once you identify what these external factors are, you will know what you need to change in order to obtain and maintain sobriety. Add any additional triggers you can think of that you haven't experienced in the past 24 hours to the list. A trigger outside of your normal routine could be a an interaction with a specific family member or an argument with your significant other.

"

'For 18 months. I hated my job. And he wasn't working. So we would fight, a lot. That would cause so much tension in the house. Even if we were both trying to stay sober. He would relapse. It was the lifestyle we were living. Hangout out. Getting high. I would get high with him, because that is what we did together. How we bonded.' **Kelly F., Michigan**

'Yea, especially when my mom would stop by. She always wanted to know how I was doing with the job search. And when I was going back to school. Therapy helped me realize that I would get high instead of planning for the future. She was high with me most of the time, so we never had those conversations. It was hard. But I got sober for myself, first. Because I knew if I stayed sober, she would.' **Jack F., Michigan**

"When I was a kid my father would come home from work and head straight to the refrigerator to have a beer, or two, or three. He would drink an entire case if there was one. And if he was out, he went straight to the store to buy more. I guess I thought that was what a man was supposed to so do, because I found myself stuck in the same routine.

I would work all day, and unwind by drinking all night. After a few beers, I didn't want to be bothered by anyone. I would just pass out on the couch and sleep until I had to wake up and go to work the next morning. I thought that was the normal way to unwind. In reality, I drank so I didn't have to deal with my life.

I was so embarrassed that I worked at a company for 10 years, and didn't have an office on Management role. I became a loner for about 2 years- didn't attend birthday parties, weddings, or even socialize at work. I wanted a wife and even kids, but drinking occupied my free time and made it nearly impossible to meet anyone or focus on my career." **Brandon, Ohio**

MY CRAVINGS AND TRIGGERS

-
-
-
-
-
-
-
-
-
-
-

-
-
-
-
-
-
-
-
-
-
-

Look at the list you just created. These are the people, places and things that have been controlling your life until this point. In some way they have each caused you to use drugs or alcohol due to the way they make you feel. You cannot change the behavior of others or the existence of certain places or things, but what you can do is change how you react to them.

To do so, you will need to identify what events in your life are responsible for the triggers and your responses to them.

◈   ◈   ◈   ◈   ◈   ◈

8

YOUR TIMELINE

Triggers of drug and alcohol use develop during both happy and sad occasions in one's life. It is time to think about the positive and negative events that led to your use, and the triggers associated with each one.

On the following pages, draw a horizontal line straight across the middle of the page. This will be the beginning of the timeline of all the events leading up to the height of your drug or alcohol use. Start on the left from age 5, and continue to the right for as many pages as you need, to outline each stage of your life. Above the line, write down all the positive events that have happened. And below the line, write the negative events. Try hard to include both positive and negative for each stage.

POSITIVE

NEGATIVE

POSITIVE

NEGATIVE

POSITIVE

NEGATIVE

POSITIVE

NEGATIVE

Now look at the negative. Have you dealt with them? Are these causing you to use? If you had a deep trauma that is still affecting you, you should consider getting professional help to help you deal with it. If these are things you can deal with, remember these events happened, but you need to plan your life and not let your past control you.

❖ ❖ ❖ ❖ ❖ ❖

9

LIKE YOURSELF

Make a list of all the positive and negative traits about yourself. Other people do not have to like you, but you must like yourself. Be honest and do not focus on all the negatives. Remember, writing down positive things will make you feel better in the future. Do not leave them out. Try to find positives in the negatives.

My Personality Traits

I am _____

I am _____

I am _____

I am _____

I am _____

I am _____

I AM FRIENDLY	**I AM LAZY**	**I AM ADVENTUROUS**	**I AM SOCIABLE**	**I AM PUNCTUAL**
I have a lot of friends and I like them	I do not like working. I like sleeping	I am brave and take risks. I like dangerous sports	I like being with people. I don't like being alone. I have many friends	I am always on time. I am never late because I care about time
I AM HARDWORKING I like working I am successful at school/work I am not lazy	**I AM TALKATIVE** I can't stop talking	**I AM PESSIMISTIC** Nothing good ever happens to me. Everything is bad	**I AM GENEROUS** I like helping others. I give to others in need	**I AM SELFISH** I do not share.
I AM UNSELFISH I like to share	**I am OPTIMISTIC** Life is beautiful. Everything always gets better	**I AM UNTIDY** I can't find anything in my house because it is a mess.	**I am SHY** I can't talk to people very easily. I need time to relax	**I am MEAN** I am not nice to others. I have a lot but will not share. I do not help others

Now we are going to change the negatives into positives.

Pick 1 negative and circle it. On the next page, write down your plan on how you will fix that today.

In your plan think about what your suck points are, where you want to go, and what you want to do with your life. How you want to get there, and what is causing this issue.

"He was a very aggressive person. Like at restaurants, if his order was wrong, he would cause a big scene. And I would do the opposite. Even if my order was wrong, I would keep it to myself, and say nothing. Neither of us got our needs met that way."
-Kelly F., Michigan

"I was a know it all. Thought I knew everything, and listened to no one. I learned that people who did not support my Lifestyle, were actually the ones who cared."
-Jack F., Michigan

I plan to stop being so _____

by _____

_____

_____

_____

_____

_____

_____

_____

_____

_____

_____

_____

_____

_____

_____

_____

_____

_____

_____

Be sure to practice changing the negatives into positives every day. Remember these negatives while you are completing each activity. You will need to work on these to accomplish any of your goals.

What about your personality is causing the problems in your life? Identify the pieces of yourself that you don't like. Write a paragraph for each trait you recognize in yourself on how you will change them.

APPearance	Personality	Feelings {Positive}	Feelings {Negative}
o adorable	o aggressive	o agreeable	o anxious
o attractive	o ambitious	o amused	o bewildered
o alluring	o brave	o brave	o clumsy
o confident	o bright	o calm	o confused
o disheveled	o clumsy	o comfortable	o defeated
o elegant	o cruel	o delightful	o depressed
o fair	o cooperative	o eager	o disappointed
o filthy	o diligent	o energetic	o disturbed
o glamorous	o determined	o excited	o embarrassed
o glowing	o fearless	o grateful	o envious
o handsome	o generous	o jolly	o fierce
o homely	o helpful	o jovial	o grumpy
o lovely	o honest	o lively	o helpless
o magnificent	o jealous	o proud	o jealous
o pleasant	o knowledgeable	o peaceful	o nervous
o perfect	o mysterious	o relieved	o somber
o scruffy	o successful	o silly	o sorrowful
o shiny	o sincere	o thankful	o troubled
o slender	o selfish	o thrilled	o vengeful
o sparkling	o talented	o victorious	o weary
o splendid	o witty	o witty	o wicked
o vivacious	o wise		
o wild	o zany		

❖ ❖ ❖ ❖ ❖ ❖

10

WHO AM I

Drug and Alcohol abuse and its consequences can be detrimental to ones self-esteem. Altering how you see yourself is crucial in Recovery. You must start seeing the good in life.

Drugs and alcohol are mind controlling substances and harm ones self worth. When addicted, you lose focus, perspective and passion that you once had. This exercise will help you to regain your sense of passion. Once you understand your passion, you will start to fill your time with joy and abundance over the mind altering substances that once took it from you.

You will do this first by identifying your passion and purpose. A necessity in achieving self-satisfaction and fulfillment. Second, you will fit into a group and engage in activities that will help you. Remember, anything is possible when you are abstinent.

What is your passion and purpose? Lets find out! Complete the following statements below.

I feel stuck because _____

_____

_____

_____

_____

_____

_____

_____

_____

_____

I keep repeating the same pattern of behavior which is

I am unhappy with my job or career because _____

I can make the same amount of money I make now and be much happier if I _____

My education level is _____ ____

I could make more money if I _____

The hours I work are _____ __ __

_____

_____

_____

_____

_____

_____

_____

I am or I am not fulfilled with what I do everyday because ____

_____

_____

_____

_____

_____

_____

_____

To change my current situation I am willing to _____

Now it's time to make your action plan. Utilizing the statements you have just written, write down the goals you would like to achieve. Your goals should put you on the path to fulfillment. When you accomplish each of your goals will you be happier than you are now. You need a plan to stay sober, focused, and disciple in order to enjoy your life.

GIVE YOURSELF AT LEAST 10 MINUTES TO COMPLETE THIS ACTIVITY

What are the goals you would like to achieve within the next <u>3 months</u>?

What are the goals you would like to achieve within the next <u>6 months</u>?

What are the goals you would like to achieve within the next **9 months**?

What are the goals you would like to achieve within the next <u>year</u>?

What are the goals you would like to achieve within the next <u>5 years</u> ?

Now Look at your goals. Do they align with what you are doing now? Think about what you can you do to work towards conquering each of your goals. Write down 5 things you will do tomorrow that you did not do today.

1. _____
_____
_____
_____
_____

2. _____
_____
_____
_____
_____

3. _____

4. _____

5. _____

◇ ◇ ◇ ◇ ◇ ◇

11

CIRCLE OF INFLUENCE

To obtain and maintain Recovery, you must closely evaluate who you interact with on a daily basis. These people both consciously and subconsciously influence who you are, how you feel, and how you behave. Let's find out who in your circle of influence is good for you and who isn't.

On the next page, write down the top 10 people you spend time with on a weekly basis This could be in over the telephone, on social media, or in person. If you have a dealer or favorite bartender they should be on this list. Add your significant other.

TOP 10 PEOPLE IN YOUR LIFE

1. _____

2. _____

3.

4.

5. _____

6. _____

7. _____

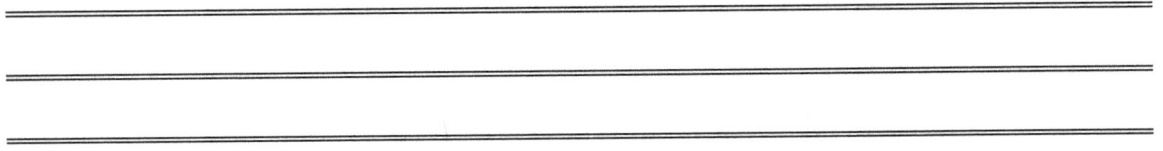

8.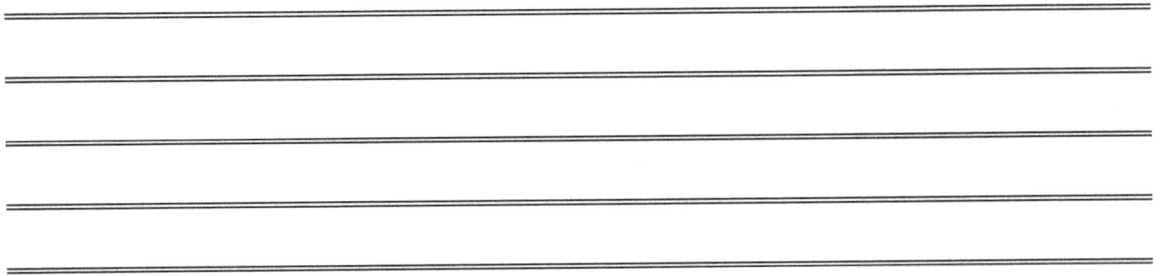

9.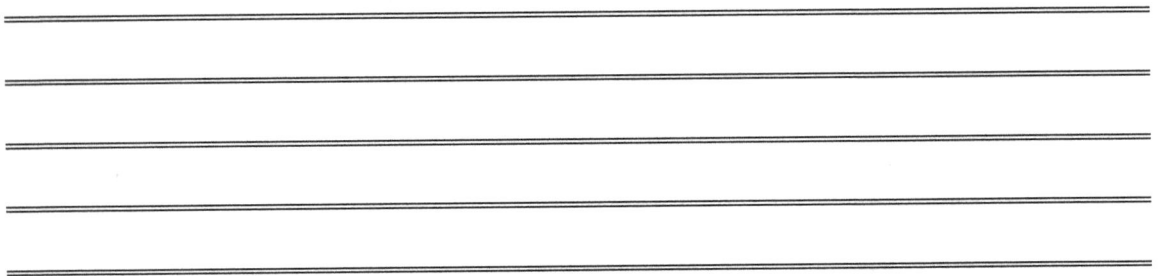

10. _____

_____

_____

_____

_____

_____

Now, go back and list the activities you routinely do with each person. Do you use drugs or alcohol with them? Do you go to the local bar together?

Circle all of the people still abusing drugs or alcohol. Circle anyone you feel is toxic in some way. Maybe they are one of your triggers. Or, perhaps you have noticed that you feed off each others negative energy. Do they cosign or enable harmful behavior? If so, circle their name.

Look at this list of people. They are influencing and making your Recovery much more difficult. Now is the time to change this. Understand that this is now your old circle of influence. Accept that you must make a change now in order to move forward in Recovery.

Look at everyone you circled. Prepare to start letting them go out of your life.

"When I stopped drinking completely, I had time. I found a new job, joined a gym, and started working out. I felt Great! And that's how I met my girlfriend Jenna who's a nutritionist. We support each other in sobriety, eat very healthy, and remain very positive for each other." **Brandon, Ohio**

Now, create new list on the next page. Write down all the people from the original list that you did not circle.

TOP TEN PEOPLE I WILL START SPENDING MORE TIME WITH

1. _____

2. _____

3. _____

4. _____

5. _____

6. _____

7. _____

8. _____

9. _____

10. _____

Now add anyone you know that seems happy and fulfilled, and write them down. Do you have a sober friend that you lost touch with? Add them.

For the next two weeks work on spending more time with these individuals. I ask that you try to stay off social media during this time. This will enable you to have more control over who you interact with. You should also look for a substance abuse support group, recreational sports team, or fitness class to help you meet new people that will have a positive influence over you and your sobriety.

You have identified your triggers, cravings, and toxic people that lead you to substance abuse. Some of these you will not be able to avoid completely. Drugs and alcohol are everywhere. You may be triggered by required family events. Or, the toxic person in your life may be your boss or spouse. In addition to limiting your interactions, you need to desensitize yourself to these influences. You need to get to the point where you are comfortable around them and not use or take a drink.

On the next page, write down all events and gatherings you were required to attend over the past year. This should include family dinners, business meetings, office parties, and weddings. Many major events are celebrated with eating and drinking.

LIST OF MANDATORY EVENTS

_____ _____   _____

_____ _____   _____

_____ _____   _____

_____ _____   _____

_____ _____   _____

_____ _____   _____

_____ _____   _____

_____ _____   _____

_____ _____   _____

_____ _____   _____

Now rate from 1 to 10 on how stressful or difficult it will be for you to attend each event sober in the future. With 1 being easy and 10 being impossible. Now circle each event that you score at a 7 or higher.

These are the events you must prepare for. If you absolutely must attend, perhaps you should leave early. Or, you can bring a supportive friend along. Prepare yourself for what is ahead, now.

Write an action plan below on how to deal with each environment and the people that will be there.

❖ ❖ ❖ ❖ ❖ ❖

12

FOOD AND SLEEP MOOD JOURNALING

Addiction recovery is all about identifying what makes you want to use drugs and alcohol, and fixing the behavior. Your past substance abuse was a coping mechanism to make you feel better. You have already started working on identifying the triggers, cravings, and other people that have any effect on your mood. And have create a plan to be in better control over those factors. So adding two more will be simple for you.

Your body responds differently to everything you eat. Similar to how different drugs or alcoholic beverages altered your behavior in specific ways. In order to control your mood, you need to better control what you eat. You need to eat what makes you feel that way you want to feel.

And another factor is sleep. Not every adult needs 8 hours of sleep every night. Some require 6. And others require 10 or more. No two people are alike. To understand what you require to feel how you want to feel, complete the following Food and Sleep mood activity. Answer the following questions.

How many hours did you sleep last night? _____

What did you eat today?

_____

_____

_____

_____

_____

How did you feel today? Did you feel Grumpy, happy, or restless? Sad or motivated? _____

Did you exercise? _____

Push yourself to answer these questions before you go to sleep everyday, for the next 7 days. Utilize the pages at the end of your journal to record your answers. As soon as you notice a negative pattern of behavior, correct it. If you had a bad day, think about how much sleep you had the night before. Did you eat fruits and vegetables, or junk food that day?

At the end of the week identify the common factors on the bad days versus on the good days. Make the decision that you deserve to have the good days outweigh the bad, and adjust your diet and sleeping habits accordingly.

◈ ◈ ◈ ◈ ◈ ◈

13

ORGANIZE YOUR BUDGET AND FINANCES

Often people who struggle with drugs and alcohol, develop a pattern of needing immediate gratification. You start spending so much money on these substances, that you stop caring if you can afford it or not. This is due to the psychological hold the drugs have over you. Now that you are in active Recovery, you will not have these expenses. You can now plan your spending. It doesn't matter how much or little you have. You still need to budget and account for it.

Write down how much you think you would spend monthly on drugs, alcohol, or anything you did not need. This would include gambling or any other partying behavior.

$_____

Now to verify this number, write a list of all the things you would spend money on due to the lifestyle you were living, and the estimated total monthly spend.

_____ $_____

_____ $_____

_____ $_____

_____ $_____

_____ $_____

_____ $_____

_____ $_____

_____ $_____

_____ $_____

_____ $_____

_____ $_____

_____ $_____

_____ $_____

_____ $_____

_____ $_____

_____ $_____

Now add them up. What is that total?

$_____

It is time for you to plan out how you will better allocate your finances going forward. Write down how much money you make in a month.

$\$\underline{\hspace{5cm}}$ - $\$\underline{\hspace{5cm}}$ =

monthly income   living expenses

Subtract your living expenses. This would be your rent or mortgage, car payment, or any child support or alimony. Subtract your food expenses, and all utility bills. How much is left?

$\$\underline{\hspace{4cm}}$

If you are not earning enough to cover your basic bills you need to reevaluate your job. Or, pick up a second or third job now that you have gained more productive hours each day due to your sobriety.

If you have money left over, congratulations. You know for the next 30 days you will have a place to live and all of your necessities taken care of, first. If you get into this habit every month, you will be less likely to use drugs or alcohol. You will be less stressed over your finances, and can focus on achieving your passions and goals. The money you have left will be allocated to fun, savings, and $20 or so can go towards a bucket list savings.

On the next page in your journal, create a bucket list of fun activities or trips that you would like to go on in the future. Rip it out, and hang it up somewhere you will see every day – like your bedroom mirror. Or, take picture of it, and add it as your cellphone background image. Utilize this list as an additional motivator to properly handle your finances, stay clear of drugs or alcohol, and make all your dreams come true.

MY BUCKET LIST

1) _____

2) _____

3) _____

4) _____

5) _____

6) _____

7) _____

8) _____

9) _____

10) _____

◇　◇　◇　◇　◇　◇

14

YOUR NEW BEGINNING

This concludes volume one of the Addiction Recovery DIY series. If you were able to follow and complete all activities while keeping your sobriety, you are well on your way in Recovery. If you stumbled, or relapsed, that is okay too. Start from the beginning of this series, and see what you can do differently. What did you miss? You may need to consider Rehab, a therapist, or life coach to help you get to the next step. And that's okay.

Either way, please always remember your goals and your bucket list. Make sure you put everything in order.

Take that leap and apply to higher paying jobs or go to school, before you can get the nicer car or house.

Focus on how hard you are willing to make these things happen, over how hard or challenging accomplishing them will be. Shift into a motivational mindset where everything is possible with abstinence.

◈　◈　◈　◈　◈　◈

◈ ◈ ◈ ◈ ◈ ◈

www.ingramcontent.com/pod-product-compliance
Lightning Source LLC
Chambersburg PA
CBHW081011040426
42443CB00016B/3485